DARE WE BE CHRISTIANS?

Dare We Be Christians?

Walter Rauschenbusch

The William Bradford Collection
from
The Pilgrim Press

SERIES EDITOR
BARBARA BROWN ZIKMUND

THE PILGRIM PRESS
CLEVELAND , OHIO

First published in 1914 by The Pilgrim Press
The William Bradford Collection edition
published 1993
by The Pilgrim Press
Foreword by Stephen G. Post © 1993
by The Pilgrim Press

Printed in the United States of America

The paper used in this publication is acid free
and meets the minimum requirements of the
American National Standard for Information
Sciences-Permanence of Paper for Printed Library
Materials, ANSI Z39. 48-1984

98 97 96 95 94 93   5 4 3 2 1

Library of Congress Cataloging-in-Publication Data
Rauschenbusch, Walter, 1861-1918.
Dare we be Christians? / Walter Rasuchenbusch.
    p. cm. — (the William Bradford collection
        from the Pilgrim Press)
        ISBN 0-8298-0960-0 (alk. paper)
    1. Love—Religious aspects—Christianity.
            2. Christian ethics.
            3. Social Ethics.
            I. Title.   II. Series
            BV4639.R35   1993
                241'.4—dc20
                93-11041 CIP

CONTENTS

FOREWORD BY STEPHEN G. POST
VII

DARE WE BE CHRISTIANS?
1

FOREWORD

In this splendid little work published in 1914, Walter Rauschenbusch, the most distinguished American "Social Gospel" theologian, interprets Christian love largely in the light of special relations such as married love, parental love, and friendship. Thus Rauschenbusch demonstrates a keen interest in the familial sphere and in so-called personal ethics that most readers will find rather surprising for a thinker known only as a champion of the laboring poor in their struggle against economic injustice.

FOREWORD

Underlying this interpretation of love is a resistance to the Kantian conception of the moral agent as ahistorical, stripped of the special relations that develop over time between those in proximity, and as abstracted from the familial ties that in reality are such a large part of everyday moral experience for most of us. Rauschenbusch was of course deeply informed by Kant in other respects. But judging from *Dare We Be Christians?* the author rejected the Kantian endeavor to transcend all empirical anthropology and human embeddedness in the phenomenal world of special relations.

Like all Christian thinkers, Rauschenbusch puts considerable emphasis on love for persons as such, for strangers in need. But such love evolves from the experience and lessons of more intimate ties, and this is where Rauschenbusch deserves very serious attention. Here is the essential significance of this important work: Christian love expands concentrically from smaller spheres of intimacy of "solidarity," to the wider sphere of humanity as such, much like a pebble cast into a smooth pond creates ripples of learned love spreading outward in all directions.

Permit me a comparison to highlight the immediate relevance of *Dare We Be Christians?* In his book *The Fall* (1957), the French existentialist Albert Camus describes an expatriate Frenchman in a seedy Amsterdam bar who confesses that due to his failures in friendship and marriage he now loves "the whole human race." (Hence the powerful French adage, "I love humanity, it is only people I detest.") Not that Camus denied the moral importance of love for humanity, but he was highly suspicious of those who proclaimed such love to the neglect of those people near and dear with whom we are naturally entrusted. Rauschenbusch seems to share this suspicion.

In reading *Dare We Be Christians?* I am also reminded of the mid-nineteenth-century American preacher William H. McGuffey, whose 1844 essay "True and False Philanthropy" was so influential on American culture. McGuffey contrasts Mr. Fantom and Mr. Goodman. Mr. Fantom begins: "I despise a narrow field. O for the reign of universal benevolence! I want to make all mankind good and happy." Mr. Goodman responds that "one must begin to love somewhere; and I think it is natural to love one's own family, and to do good in one's own neighborhood, as to anybody else." Mr. Goodman laments of Mr. Fantom, "and so, between the great thing he cannot do, and the little one that he will not do, life passes, and nothing will be done." Such common sense may have held Rauschenbusch in the real world of love despite the temptation to abstraction.

The reader of *Dare We Be Christians?* may take note of the remarkable section titled "The Scope of Love in Society." There, the author begins his discussion with deep appreciation of the love between man and woman. He refers to intense joy and to the agony of unrequital or of trust broken: he reflects on a "physical and mental intimacy of life which binds them in a lasting social partnership of work and mutual care. If it were not an old story it would be a miracle." And this miracle of love "is always weaving new combinations of lives," as whole groups of families are connected ideally in "friendly cooperation." But even more miraculous, from this conjugal union love "springs forward to bond young and mature in a new and amazing bond." Here Rauschenbusch is elegant and inspired, proclaiming that "the love of fatherhood and motherhood is a divine revelation and a miracle. It is a creative act of God in us." The moral character of the self changes profoundly as "the water of sacrificial love pours forth." (I am reminded of my sister's compliment some years ago that she never really liked me until I became a father.) Without this fountainhead of human society, "children would die like the flies of later summer and the race would perish."

While Rauschenbusch views family affections as the most powerful and striking forms of love because they have "the support of physical nearness and of constant intercourse and habit," he takes deep interest in goodwill toward the "chance-met stranger." The theme of love's expansion is paramount: "So the love for one man promptly widens out into the love of many and weaves more closely the web of social life." All social progress is love widened from its first dawn in the love of "parent animals for their young" to "common blood and the sense of kinship" to love for humanity as a whole. But this last step is linked to Jesus' teaching to his "friends" that God is a parent who loves all children, and we must therefore love all humanity if we claim to love God.

There is no doubt room for some criticism of Rauschenbusch from the perspective

FOREWORD

of current Christian theology. Many theologians have moved beyond God the Father to a dyadic theism of the Mother-Father God or to a gender-neutral description of God in terms of Being or First Cause. Many have moved to a progressive notion of gender-role equity, liberating women from the tyranny of patriarchy. So *Dare We Be Christians?* can be dismissed, although it clearly should not be. Rauschenbusch was a man of his times, subject to the intellectual barriers of his era. In his defense, Rauschenbusch does see the love of both motherhood and fatherhood as divine revelation. His brief treatise on love should not be read as a defense of conservative or patriarchal "family values," for surely Rauschenbusch heralded advances in equality and true mutuality.

This study must be appreciated for the author's unique and powerful articulation of Christian love against the background of human nature as he understood it. Agape is grounded in, and expands outward from, basic human affections. This is a welcome relief from theories of agape that begin with love for humanity and have either very little or nothing to say about the special relations that make human life possible and in which most of our moral development occurs.

Dare We Be Christians? is a minor classic on Christian love, and the republication of this work is a significant event in the literature. It deserves to be read seriously as an elegant corrective message to contemporary Christian ethics, since theologians informed by Kierkegaard, Anders Nygren, and many other theorists of agape either ignore special relations or view them as obstacles rather than roads to love for humanity. If every Christian ethicist—nay, every Christian—reads this little book, it will be a little better world.

STEPHEN G. POST
Department of Religion
Case Western Reserve University

Dare We Be Christians?

God's world is great; too great for a little
mind like mine to hold. I have traveled over
thousands of miles of it, but for the most part
my memory holds only a blur of space and
movement.

But there are a few places which my
memory has made all my own. I know a
place, just above Little Mud Turtle Lake,
where the Gull River tilts around the rocks
and sweeps in a curling crescent of foam
around the wooded basin below the rapids.
That place is mine because I swam in it with
my boys; the river carried us down the
rapids and around the whirlpool, shouting

and laughing. 'Way up on the Ox Tongue River is a high, straight fall, and above it a platform of rock. I lay there one night in the open, while the cool night wind moved the treetops, and watched the constellations march across the spaces between them. That place is mine by the emotions and prayers it inspired.

The world of the Bible, too, is a great world. I have wandered through it all, but I have never made it all my own. But some friendly hills and valleys in it are mine by right of experience. Some chapters have comforted me; some have made me homesick; some have braced me like a bugle call; and some always enlarge me within by a sense of unutterable fellowship with a great, quiet Power that pervades all things and fills me.

Such passages make up for each of us his Bible within the Bible, and the extent and variety of these claims he has staked out in it measure how much of the great Book has really entered into the substance of his life.

DARE WE BE CHRISTIANS?

PAUL'S PRAISE OF LOVE

Some passages are common camping ground for us all. The thirteenth chapter of Paul's First Letter to the Corinthians is one of these. That half-page of print has been a force in human history. If we could follow its course through the generations, we should find it marked, like the windings of a brook, by a special greenness of life, by ferns and buttercups and gentians and cardinal flowers of human kindness. It has set the mired runnels of good-will flowing again. It has gentled our resentful feelings and made us forgiving. By making us feel the worth of love, it has made us feel the worth of those we ought to love. The old psalm ascribes to the pilgrim saints of God the capacity to "pass through the valley of weeping" and leave it "a place of springs." This saintly little chapter has done just that by its irrigation of affection and cleansed will.

It has such power to move us because it moved Paul deeply as he wrote it. His sen-

3

tences suddenly grow rhythmic. His style runs into prose-poetry. His language rocks with the wave-beat of emotion. He was sure of a similar response from the Christian hearts to whom he was writing. This chapter is first-class evidence that primitive Christianity was charged with a high voltage of human affection and social enthusiasm, for this Christian man was shaken with deep feeling as soon as he began to touch on this live subject that was sure and common ground for the Christian consciousness.

The chapter is also documentary evidence of inspiration. Here we can watch inspiration in the very act and see the spirit of Christ bearing up the flutterings of the human mind with the sweep of mightier wings.

EMOTIONAL RELIGION

Paul apparently had not intended to write this chapter. It came to him while he was discussing the vexed question of "spiritual gifts." In aftertimes Christianity came to mean largely creeds, rituals, rules, holy buildings and priests—a sort of religion at second hand with a reflected light and warmth. But in the first generation it came over men as a power direct from the unseen world; as a new and sweet vitality that melted their hearts with a glow of divine love and overwhelmed the baser passions of the past; as a revelation and vision that made their intellect clairvoyant, creating an insight and foresight that transcended the mental powers of which they had previously been conscious, inspiring prayers and longings so intense and lofty that they seemed to hear God's own spirit groaning in travail within their breasts. Such spiritual life was fertile in manifold expressions. The Christians called them "spiritual gifts" and classified them.

Now, when religion comes over a whole community with this elemental force, it is not an unmixed blessing. The power that establishes the souls of the strong may unhinge the minds of the weak. Look around and you will find plenty of men and women who do not realize God in the life-giving power of the sunshine and the daily goodness of life, but who do realize him in thunderstorms, earthquakes and sudden blessings. Religion for them begins beyond the boundary line of the normal, and becomes the more divine the more abnormal it is. They take joy in yielding their emotions and their intellect to mysterious powers and abdicating the possession of their own personality in favor of uncontrollable psychic forces.

There was one "gift" called "tongues." According to the traits mentioned by Paul in the fourteenth chapter it was a form of utterance with a maximum of emotion and a minimum of reason, cries and croonings that seemed repellent and insane to outsiders and unintelligible to Christians, and that left no clear thought even in the minds of those who spoke in "tongues." But it was no doubt very wonderful to those who took this plunge into the perfumed cataract of religious emotions.

Some at Corinth were in doubt about this matter, as they well might be, and asked Paul to advise them. He took up the subject formally in the twelfth chapter. He pleaded for a broad-minded tolerance of all the "varieties of religious experience." "There are varieties of talents, but the same Spirit; varieties of service, but the same Lord; varieties of effects, but the same God who effects everything in everyone." As the richly-organized life of the human body depends on the manifoldness of its members and of their functions, so with the social body of a Christian community.

SOCIAL UTILITY IN RELIGION

Thus Paul, as usual, stands for the broader and more inclusive attitude. But it is well worth noting that he pleads for this toleration, not because every individual has an inherent right to the expression of his peculiar religious experiences and ideas, but because the interaction of many different capacities will in the end serve the common good. Paul is the patron saint of all modern religious individualists; his writings are their chief reliance in the Bible. Yet here he applies the test of social utility to the most intimate expression of religious life. He argues that religious diversity and individualism are good because they serve the community.

This social estimate of religious endowments involves another thought which he brings out in the fourteenth chapter—namely that the various gifts must rank high or low in the Christian estimate according to the degree of their serviceableness to all. He held that "prophesying" was far better than "speaking with tongues," because it was rational, intelligible to all and sure to educate the Christian intelligence of the whole group, while "speaking with tongues" at most blessed him who spoke, but wasted the time and opportunity of the rest. So he demands that the needs of the community shall have the right of way over private religious pleasures, and advises those who "speak with tongues" to do it in the privacy of their own prayers.

This was very clever of Paul. Most of the abnormal and highly-wrought manifestations of religion suck their strength from popular notice and admiration. Isolate them and they wilt. Paul did here for religious emotionalism what Jesus did for the religious formalism of the Pharisees, when he advised them to take their long prayers into their closets and see how much would be left of them if God alone took notice of them.

In favoring prophesying over "speaking with tongues" Paul prefers religion *plus* reason to religion *minus* reason—a principle of immense practical importance. And here again he takes the social ground that religion which has utility for the community is better than religion which serves only personal needs, even if the latter seems the more wonderful and inspired.

Thus we have in the twelfth and fourteenth chapters two main lines of thought: first, that the Christian Church can tolerate a large diversity of religious forces and forms of expression, provided they all serve the common good; second, that those forms of religion rank highest which are most completely under the direction of reason and most serviceable to the whole group.

I repeat that the precision with which Paul brings out this social criterion in religious questions is unstudied evidence of the strong social force set free by the Christian religion. Paul often asserted that every act of a Christian man should be upborne by religious impulses; even when we eat and drink we should do so "in Christ" and "to the glory of God." But here he sticks to the reverse of this just as tenaciously, affirming that all religious life must have social utility and that its value is measured by its social qualities.

10

DARE WE BE CHRISTIANS?

Now it had apparently been in Paul's mind to pass directly from the discussion in the twelfth chapter about the manifoldness of spiritual gifts to the second part of the discussion, in the fourteenth chapter, about the superior value of prophesying. He was about to make the transition in the thirty-first verse: "Set your mind on the higher gifts"; that is, so far as you have a choice, cultivate those spiritual experiences which will be most fruitful to all. He later has to come back to this transitional thought at the beginning of the fourteenth chapter: "Follow after love; yet desire earnestly spiritual gifts, especially the gift of prophesying."

AN INSPIRED INTERRUPTION

But the smooth progress of his argument is interrupted. A still more important thought demands the right of way. "Hold! Listen! There is something still higher and more excellent. All speaking with tongues, all prophesying, all religious insight, all

11

miracle-working faith, all alms-giving, all the heroism of martyrdom, are condemned to futility unless love is an ingredient in them."

This unintentional origin of Paul's praise of love is to me one of the most suggestive facts about it. One of the most beautiful and powerful religious utterances in all literature thus rose spontaneously from a Christina soul. It is as if an angel had touched him on the shoulder and said: "Speak the final word, Paul! Tell them the greatest thing of all." So here we catch inspiration in the act. The quiet, logical march of the argument was burst apart by a thought so divine and insistent that it could not wait, and that thought was the indispensableness of love in religion.

But in reality it was no interruption. Inspiration does not paralyze reason but intensifies it; it does not tear up the track of true argument, but lifts argument to higher levels. In form this praise of love is an interlude, an intermezzo in *adagio cantabile;* in substance it was the real climax of the whole reasoning. The fundamental Christian consciousness of Paul demanded utterance and everything else had to stand aside. The discussion about the relative value of tongues and prophesying, which was to have been the culmination, becomes a mere corollary after Christ has spoken in Paul.

For the emphasis on love was that spiritual strain which he had most directly derived from the Master himself. To Jesus the law of love was so great and all-inclusive that he felt it summed up and superseded the whole majestic framework of the Jewish law. Jesus transformed the inherited conceptions of God himself by baptizing the Hebrew Jehovah in love and reintroducing the imperious King of Sinai to humanity as the Father whom they might love because he loved them to the death. So it was the inspiration of the spirit of Christ which spoke up in Paul when he paused to assert that love is the last and best word of life and the indispensable ingredient of all that claims to be Christian.

Does Paul, then, at this highest point of his argument turn his back on the demand for social utility which he expressed in the other parts? On the contrary. In demanding love he demands social solidarity. Love is the social instinct, the power of social coherence, the *sine qua non* of human society. In putting his hand on love as the essential thing in the Christian life, he laid hold at the same time of the most important thing in all social philosophy. For if there were no love there would be no sociology.

WE NEED A MODERN SUPPLEMENT

The supreme value of love emerged in Paul's mind when he was looking for a clear landmark to guide himself and his Corinthian friends across the uncharted sea of emotional religion. Now, the specific questions with which he had to deal have become obsolete. The "spiritual gifts" died out in the second or third generation, as they have always died out gradually in later inspirational Christian bodies. Few of us have ever heart anyone speak in "tongues." But love is as great and indispensable as ever. The demand that religion shall be socially fruitful has been taken up by all the world today with an insistent cry that has shaken the Church and has produced an overhauling of all its life.

We ought to see the indispensableness of love amid the facts of the twentieth century with the same precision and the same Christian enthusiasm as Paul saw it in the first century. We have a long historical perspective of nineteen hundred years where Paul had only the clouded mirror of prophetic foresight. We have the vast horizon of modern international relations, the huge conflicts of social forces, against which we must see the need of love, whereas Paul lived in the main within the slender groups of Christians scattered through Asia Minor and

Greece, focussing their interests intensely, and seeing all the other mighty social forces of the Roman Empire only as the dark and heaving background of Christian martydom and triumph.

It is no great evidence of Christian faith and inspiration if we rehearse Paul's points of view and misinterpret our world by superimposing his world over it. Have we faith enough to believe that the Christian doctrine of love is the solution of our big modern questions? Do we dare to assert the futility of everything in our great world of commerce and industry that leaves love out? Do we dare to undertake the readjustment of all social life to bring it into obedience to the law of love? That is a far severer test of our faith in Christ than to believe in the infallibility of a book or in the certainty of dogmas formulated so long ago that only a few hundred men in Christendom today know what they originally were meant to mean.

16

DARE WE BE CHRISTIANS?

We need a modern supplement to Paul's praise of love, written in the face of present-day problems and with a twentieth-century point of view, but with the same old Christian enthusiasm for love and the same old faith in the power of Jesus Christ to inspire love. I have not Paul's mind. I have neither the severe consistency of his reasoning nor the swift terseness of his phrases nor the blazing heat of his sacrificial enthusiasm—and it seems an amusing work of supererogation even to disavow any such thought. But I take him at his word—that "there are diversities of gifts but the same spirit"—and propose to write a few varieties on his *Leitmotif*, which he, in turn, got from our common Master.

THE SCOPE OF LOVE IN SOCIETY

In order to understand the place of love in human life we must first understand the scope of the word we use, the manifoldness and reach of the force we are to discuss.

DARE WE BE CHRISTIANS?

Whenever the Christian religion comes to a new people, it finds the native vocabulary defective for its special purposes. In the rich vocabulary of the Greek language it could find plenty of words to express hate, but none that signified humility without casting on it the slur of servility, and none that signified love without a taint of sexual suggestiveness. When King James' Version was made for the English the translators of this chapter took refuge in the frosty word "charity" as more ecclesiastical, safe and proper. The men who made the Revised Version in 1881 risked the plain English "love," but even yet the idea of sex dominates the involuntary associations of ideas which it drags along with it.

The attraction between man and woman is indeed the most striking and stirring form of love. We can gauge its force by the intense joy of its satisfactions, and the agony when love is unrequited or its trust wronged or its faithfulness broken. Two persons, at oppo-

18

site poles in their physical tastes, their aesthetic habits, their aims in life, perhaps strangers to each other until recently, break away from their family bonds of a lifetime and enter into a physical and mental intimacy of life which binds them in a lasting social partnership of work and mutual care. If it were not an old story it would be a miracle. Even its reflected sensations are so charming that we never tire of reading love stories or discreetly watching them in real life.

But the love of the sexes is only a specialized form of that larger love which pervades our race. The absorbing interest that lovers take in each other is only an enrichment and intensification of that purely human interest which we take in any person we like. The more of that general interest there is fused with the special passion, the nobler and more durable will it be. If there is nothing but sex-desire we call it vice. As Tolstoi has finely said, a man loves his wife purely if he

19

thinks of her as his sister as well as his wife.

The institution of the family places upon sex-love a heavy load of work and obligation, and so tames it. Society practically says to sex-desire what Paul said to emotional religion: "Thou must be socially useful or thou shalt get no respect or countenance from us. If thou wilt form a co-operative group for service and bear children for humanity, we will honor and protect; if not, we will punish." There are some who think it would be wiser to take the saddle, the bit and the bridle from this vagrant and restless and greedy desire, letting it bear only such social obligations as it chooses and as long as it chooses. I do not care to live long enough to see that.

Through the attraction of man and maid love is always weaving new combinations of lives, reaching out to the right and the left and knitting threads that had no connections before, bringing whole groups of families into friendly cooperation and laughing at the efforts of the proud to isolate themselves from the rest of their kind.

At the same time love is preparing to connect the present and the future generations. To lovers their love seems their own peculiar joy and apart from all the world. But Humanity stands in the shadow behind them and lifts the majestic hands of blessing above them. The indomitable spirit of the race is reaching out in them toward the better days that are to be and is flinging a new defiance to death as they affirm life together.

Out of their union buds the next generation of men, and at once love springs forward to bind the young and the mature in a new and amazing bond. The love of fatherhood and motherhood is a divine revelation and miracle. It is a creative act of God in us. Last year it was not; this year it is, and all things are changed. The dry rock of our selfishness has been struck and the water of sacrificial love pours forth. The thorn-bush

21

is aflame with a beautiful fire that does not consume. The springing up of this new force of love is essential for the very existence of human society. Unless it were promptly forthcoming, children would die like the flies of later summer and the race would perish.

These family affections are the most striking and powerful forms of human love. They have the support of physical nearness and of constant intercourse and habit. But the social impulse of the race is just as truly at work in the keen interest we take in a chance-met stranger, in the cheer we feel in meeting a boyhood friend, in the sense of comradeship with those who work or play alongside of us. Every normal man has uncounted relations of good-will, and the mobility of modern life has immensely increased the contacts for most of us.

Love takes on as many forms in society as life assumes in vegetation. When it turns toward the strong and noble we call it admiration. When it turns down toward the helpless we call it pity and compassion. The sense of obligation and sympathy that draws young men and women to share the life of the poor or the backward races is love. The loyalty we feel for the great leaders in politics or war, for the masters of science, poetry, or wisdom, is a specialized form of love.

Almost every personal relation of affection connects us with a group of people who have the same interest or who are somehow identified with persons whom we love. So the love for one man promptly widens out into the love of many and weaves more closely the web of social life.

But many of our loves are directly for groups and organizations of men—for our church, our lodge, our fraternity, our college, our party. All such relationships are strong in just the degree in which they evoke love. The cohesion of selfishness is brittle. Selfishness sticks while it feeds, and then wipes its mouth and turns away. Love alone creates enduring loyalties and persuades the individual to give up something of his own for the common good of society. Therefore all organizations cultivate loyalty and the team spirit. "The team spirit" is a modern name for the wider, cooperative love.

Still larger than these selective group-relations is the patriotic enthusiasm for city, state, and country. In times of common peril or deliverance we realize the enormous power of this vast collective love, which shakes men with fierce emotion and sends them to wounds, sickness and death. Here, too, love is the real cement of society. The state has the right and power of coercion, but any state that relies chiefly on force is perishable and doomed. Republics may be slovenly and ill-prepared, but they have great staying powers in war, because they are sustained by the love of the people. No state can afford to disregard the disaffection of a large class or the work of any party that substitutes sullenness and contempt for patriotic pride.

Thus love widens out from the jealous desire of a lover who monopolizes the caresses of his beloved, to the large devotion of the great lovers of mankind and the leaders of humane causes. The firm mouth and strong jaws of Washington's portraits do not symbolize love to us like the tender face of the Madonna brooding over her child, but the steadfast devotion with which he lifted his country and his cause through years of strain and fear was an equally sublimated type of love, the love of a strong man who serves his country.

In all its forms love creates an enjoyment of contact and a desire for more of it, a sense of the worth and human beauty of those we love, pride in their advancement, joy in their happiness, pain in their suffering, a consciousness of unity, an identity of interests, an instinctive realization of solidarity.

This is the wide sense in which we must use the word "love" if we are to realize the incomparable power and value of love in human life. Our understanding of life depends on our comprehension of the universal power of love. Our capacity to build society depends on our power of calling out love. Our faith in God and Christ is measured by our faith in the value and workableness of love.

LOVE AND SOCIAL PROGRESS

Every step of social progress demands an increase in love. The history of evolution is a history of the appearance and the expansion of love. The first dawn of social cohesion appears in the love of parent animals for their young. The sympathetic type emerges as we ascend the scale of life. The offspring of love survive, propagate, and bequeath their capacity for love. Nature, by the power of life and death, weeds out the loveless and increases the totality of love in the universe.

In the history of man social organization began in groups that had common blood and

26

the sense of kinship to bind them. Every enduring enlargement of political organization demands a basis of fellow-feeling, and love as well as common economic interests. Kings and statesmen have tried to patch nations and races together by treaties or coercion, but unless intermarriage has fused the blood, and religion and common suffering have welded the spirits of the people, empires have dropped apart again along the ancient lines of cleavage. The history of the Germans, the Italians and the Slavs in the nineteenth century and today consists largely of the effort to undo the artificial cobbling and stitching of kingcraft and to allow the nations to coalesce in commonwealths along the lines marked out by national love and race coherence.

We can watch the society-making force of love at work in the creation of new social organizations. Not even a little local trade union nor lodge nor church nor club can be made successful unless there are in its membership some individuals with the higher qualities of enthusiasm and affection. Selfish interests are necessary, too, for durability, but love is the real chemical for amalgamation.

Where new organizations have to overcome resistance and hostility, as in the case of new religious movements or in the labor movement and socialism, the common suffering and the need of sympathetic support of mind by mind create a wonderful fund of fraternal love. Perhaps from the larger point of view of God the selfish opposition of those who resist the movements of the people may be justified by the fact that the labor and suffering which they impose upon the lower classes evokes love and creates solidarity— much as the travail and toil of childbearing binds the mother to her child—and so fits the new social group for future control.

Cooperative organizations are a remarkable demonstration of the society-making power of love. Judged from a financial point of view they have no chance of survival.

DARE WE BE CHRISTIANS?

Those who organize them usually have little capital, little experience, little business ability. The cooperatives are matched against the best survivors of capitalistic competition, and their entrance into the field often causes a united effort of all their competitors to keep them down, while they themselves are forbidden by their principles to undersell the others. Yet with proper management they have slowly built up an international success that commands the increasing admiration of social students. Their strength is in love. They succeed best among the lower classes, who always have to practice interdependence. They utilize strong neighborly feeling, the good-will of old acquaintanceship and kinship, or the new loyalty of socialist convictions, and the hatred for exploitation. They do not succeed among classes where every man is for himself, intent on advancing personally and quite willing to leave others behind. The next fifty years will see a long contest for survival and dominion between the capitalistic and the cooperative type of organization. The former is strong through selfishness and possession; the latter through the resources of love.

Thus love is the society-making force. Social progress depends on the available supply of love. If the sense of solidarity is so strong that injustice and oppression are intolerable to all and the creation of new fraternal relations is swift and easy, then society can efficiently meet every new strain. If one large class has no fellow-feeling and conscious regard for another large class, a flaw runs through the girder and it may split under pressure.

THE BREAKDOWN OF LOVE

This is exactly the situation which confronts us in the industrial world in all nations, including our own. Love has failed between great social classes of men. The working class have become doubtful of the identity of interest between them and the employing and possessing class. They feel they are being victimized and not led. They lag in their work. The spontaneous capacities of labor evoked by love lie dormant in them. They feel that they are hirelings and not friends of those who control their lives. They believe the share of the collective wealth which is paid over to them is determined by their own weakness and the legal and economic power of the opposing group, and not by the productive value of their work nor by their human needs.

This interpretation of their relations may be mistaken in detail. Where love is lacking, the atmosphere becomes clouded with suspicion and misunderstandings, and it becomes increasingly hard to see the truth, even for those who desire to see it. But where the area of hostility is so wide, the feeling so bitter, and the fundamental charge of injustice so frequently and clearly substantiated, no excuse or counter-charge can settle the question any longer. Jesus says if we become conscious that our brother has a grievance against us, it becomes the prime concern of our mind to make the matter right. Even if the consciousness comes to us when we are engaged in the most solemn and reverential act of religion, we are to drop everything and first heal the broken fellowship and establish love. The upper classes throughout the world are in that position. Their right of occupation and the justice of their stewardship are under challenge. The gravest issue is not simply a question of dollars and cents, but of the sterilization of love by social injustice. If love is really as important to God and humanity as we have said, this social antagonism becomes a very serious thing to a religious mind. Must we permanently live in a loveless industrial world, or do we dare to be Christians?

The frequency with which our communities have to fall back on physical coercion is a symptom of the failure of love, for love can usually dispense with force. The more love, the less force; the more force, the less love. Despotic government had to use plentiful force to keep its unnatural structure erect. The spread of democracy has brought a great softening of the horrors of criminal law and it will yet bring us a great lessening of militarism. Every proposed increase in police force and military organization is a challenge and accusation against those institutions of society which ought to create social solidarity. If ever our country draws toward its ruin, it will bristle with efficient arsenals and hired fighters. The constant use of military violence in labor disputes in our country proves that industry is still in the despotic stage. It needs democratizing and Christianizing.

LOVE AND MODERN BUSINESS

The severest test and the most urgent task of love today is in the field of business life. Unless love can dominate the making of wealth, the wealth of our nation will be the ferment of its decay. There will be no genuine advance for human society until business experiences the impulse, the joy, and the mental fertility of free teamwork. As long as industry is built on fundamental antagonisms and the axle of every wheel is hot with smothered resentment, there can be no reign of love and no new era of civilization. Our age is asking the leaders of the business world to take a great constructive forward step and to found business on organized love. It summons them to be Christians in business. It seems like a leap in the dark. Will they dare?

Every great engineering work is financed by the stored labor of the past. In the same way all moral progress must draw on the reservoir of righteous purpose and human sympathy stored by religion. Is there enough love in our nation to back up a great moral advance?

Whoever utilizes a woman to satisfy his desires, without respecting her soul and her equal human worth, prostitutes her. Whoever utilizes a man to satisfy his desire for wealth, without respecting his soul and his equal human worth, and without realizing the beating heart and hopes of his fellow, prostitutes him. Whoever gives the consent of his mind to getting unearned gain, to getting more from his fellows than he returns to them in service, steps outside of the realm of love. If the law protects semi-predatory undertakings it involves all the citizens of a democracy in wrong-doing. If the Church looks on injustice without holy anger it allows the institution of redemptive love to give shelter to lovelessness, and is itself involved in the charge of hypocrisy.

Paul laid on religion the indispensableness of love. The Christian Church must lay the same law on modern business. Thus:

If I create wealth beyond the dream of past ages and increase not love, my heat is the flush of fever and my success will deal death.

Though I have foresight to locate the fountains of riches, and power to preempt them, and skill to tap them, and have no loving vision for humanity, I am blind.

Though I give of my profits to the poor and make princely endowments for those who toil for me, if I have no human fellowship of love with them my life is barren and doomed.

Love is just and kind. Love is not greedy and covetous. Love exploits no one; it takes no unearned gain; it gives more than it gets. Love does not break down the lives of others to make wealth for itself; it makes wealth to build the life of all. Love seeks solidarity; it tolerates no divisions; it prefers equal workmates; it shares its efficiency. Love enriches all men, educates all men, gladdens all men.

The values created by love never fail; but whether there are class privileges, they shall fail; whether there are millions gathered, they shall be scattered; and whether there are vested rights, they shall be abolished. For in the past strong men lorded it in ruthlessness and strove for their own power and pride, but when the perfect social order comes, the strong shall serve the common good. Before the sun of Christ brought in the dawn, men competed, and forced tribute from weakness, but when the full day shall come, they will work as mates in love, each for all and all for each. For now we see in the fog of selfishness, darkly, but then with social vision; now we see our fragmentary ends, but then we shall see the destinies of the race of God sees them. But now abideth honor, justice, and love, these three; and the greatest of these is love.

DARE WE BE CHRISTIANS?

LOVE VALIDATES ITSELF

Love carries its own validation. It proves its own efficiency and trustworthiness in action. Selfishness always looks safe; love always looks like an enormous risk. But many a man has found that when all his other securities had depreciated, love still paid dividends. Those who are too timid to embark in some venture of love are finally left on the desert shores of a life without interest or hope.

We never live so intensely as when we love strongly. We never realize ourselves so vividly as when we are in the full glow of love for others.

Love establishes the fullest intellectual contact with the world about us. It has a passionate desire for full comprehension, whereas selfishness loses interest as soon as it has made the other serve its ends. To understand things and people we must love them. Love is the greatest educator, the most permanent stimulus of the intellectual life.

DARE WE BE CHRISTIANS?

The animals that stand out among others by
their intelligence—the dog, the ant, the bee,
the elephant—are all social and gregarious
beings; a beast that lives a solitary life must
have incessant training to learn a few poor
tricks. A selfish person becomes a stupid
person if he lives long enough. Other things
being equal, the loving people are the wise
people. Selfishness grinds a thin edge on the
mind but this edge turns and then makes a
ragged cut. Love has the keenest insight and
yet does not hurt. Selfish cleverness sees
keenly the surface mechanisms of life which
it wants to manipulate; love instinctively
imparts the deeper secrets and larger mean-
ings of God's world. The light of true wisdom does not fall on the facts of life from any
outward source; it is shed only from the
inner eye of him who beholds them, and if his
inner eye is darkened, there is no wisdom in
all the world for him.

Love demands sacrifice, and sacrifice
seems the denial and surrender of life. Actu-

ally love is the great intensifier of life and giving our life preserves it. By seeking life selfishly, we lose it; when we lose it for love we gain it. We are far more active and self-assertive when we impart than when we receive. It is literally true that "it is more blessed to give than to receive."

When people have lived for forty years and their desires begin to flag, the great test of age arrives. If they have launched young bodies and minds on the great adventurous cruise of life, there are still for them the hoisting of pennants, the slap of the open sea, the foreboding of the storm, the pride of the successful homeward run. If they have identified themselves for years with some cause of humanity—the cause of temperance or purity or peace or justice—working for it and suffering for it, their lives will have a meaning and a hope and a great pride to the end. But if they have fed no life but their own, have no investments except dollars and must pay for all the sympathy they get, they are

40

locked in a gray prison which they have built for themselves. Such lives are truly old, even if their bodies are kept young by all the skill that money buys. They have lost the fundamental contacts with the world. If we knew the profound loneliness and monotony of many people who have preferred wealth to the burdens and risks of love, we should not dash for the bait which they gorged.

On the other hand love rejuvenates life. When, occasionally, old people take a new plunge into love, they grow so young and dapper that everybody laughs. We can watch the same wonder when a child comes to people who have longed for one for years. So love is the fountain of youth which the Spanish conquistadores sought. It was located in America after all, but, being "conquerors," they could never have found it.

Jesus said that love is the supreme law of life and the thing men live by. Love validates the assertion. It pays as it goes. Nothing else does pay in the long run. The more true happiness and abiding satisfaction we have had from love, the more ought we to trust it as the true way of life.

THE OUTCOME

If, now, love is so all-pervasive and manifold in the life of humanity; if it is indeed the indispensable condition for the existence and progress of society; if it has proved its constructive value and superior efficiency whenever it has received a fair test, then I ask all who have followed these thoughts to the end to affirm with me their faith in love and to make a new committal to the cause of establishing love on earth. We must not only accept it and enjoy it when it comes to us, but we must seek it, cultivate it and propagate it like health, wealth and education. It is not an incidental blessing, but the first and fundamental law of God, written in our hearts, and written large in all the world about us. When we heal love that has been torn, remove all contradictions of

love from the outward relations of our life
and allow love to become our second nature,
we shall deserve the highest patent of nobil-
ity—to be called sons of God. If love involves
loss, we must accept the loss. Christ did. If
selfishness seems to work better than love,
we must have faith in love. Just as a business
man invests money for years in a business
proposition because he has faith in it, so we
must stake our fortune on love and feel sure
of coming out ahead in the venture. Why else
do we call ourselves Christians?

LOVE AND CHRISTIANITY

From this sunlit hill-top of reflection we
may gain a fresh vision of the significance of
Christianity.

A man is a Christian in the degree in
which he shares the spirit and consciousness
of Jesus Christ, conceiving God as Jesus
knew him and seeing human life as Jesus
realized it. None of us has ever done this
fully, but on the other hand there is no man

43

within the domain of Christendom who has not been influenced by Christ in some way.

Now Jesus with incomparable spiritual energy set love into the center of religion. He drove home the duty of love with words so mighty that our race can never again forget them. He embodied the principle of love in the undying charm and youthful strength of his own life in such a way as to exert an assimilating compulsion over more lives than we can number. He was conscious of God as a sunny and lovable presence and he taught his friends to think of God as a father who loved them unselfishly and wanted nothing from them except love. This conception of God was reenforced when men saw in the cross the great declaration of the redemptive love of God.

As the outcome of the life and death of Jesus, a body of organized life and thought was set in motion through history which interpreted the universe from the point of view of love and saw all ethical questions and duties with love at the center. If this movement had died out in the second century but its literature had been preserved, all thoughtful men today, of every school of philosophy, would point to it as the fairest and most brilliant venture ever made in the field of morals and religion. But it did not die. It has such religious vitality and organizing force that it survived and spread. Though only a fragment of its original faith was dissolved and embodied in the institutions of society, it made the nations that adopted it the dominant nations of the earth. Every time that faith was cleansed of its foreign contaminations, every time more of its force was released and embodied in social life, the history of Western civilization dated a new epoch. In spite of all failures the Christian religion has been the one organized force in the Western world which has consciously sought to increase love.

Christianity stands for the belief that "God is love." It has succeeded in making that tremendous assertion of faith a commonplace. In so far as we have taken that doctrine seriously it has revolutionized our spiritual outlook and put a new face on the universe.

Christianity stands for the doctrine that we must love one another—all men, without distinction of "religion, race, color or previous condition of servitude." It will tolerate no exempt breed of supermen and no preempted areas of God's common world. It does not call on the strong to climb to isolation across the backs of the weak, but challenges them to prove their strength by lifting the rest with them. It does not advise eliminating the unfit, but seeks to make them fit. It stands for the solidarity of the race in its weakness and strength, its defeats and conquests, its sin and salvation.

If love is the greatest thing in the world and if it is the prime condition of social progress, what of the Christian religion, which has identified itself with faith in love?

DARE WE BE CHRISTIANS?

Every man can profit by the historical influences of Christianity and be a passive pensioner on its vested funds. But it clearly needs active personal agents who will incarnate its vitalities, propagate its principles, liberate its undeveloped forces, purify its doctrine and extend the sway of its faith in love over new realms of social life. Dare we be such men? Dare we be Christians? Those who take up the propaganda of love and substitute freedom and fraternity for coercion and class differences in social life are the pioneers of the Kingdom of God; for the reign of the God of love will be fulfilled in a life of humanity organized on the basis of solidarity and love.